MICHAEL
JACKSON
FACTS FROM THE DANCEFLOOR

PHOTOGRAPHIC CREDITS

FRONT COVER © REX FEATURES

© ALL ACTION
(Pages: 27, 35, 39, 42, 43, 48, 51, 58, 67, 68, 70, 71, 72)

© LONDON FEATURES INTERNATIONAL LTD
(Pages: 6, 7, 8, 9, 10, 13, 16, 24, 36, 40, 45, 66)

© PICTORIAL PRESS
(Pages: 14, 19, 21, 23, 29, 30, 32, 33, 38, 46, 52)

© REX FEATURES
(Pages: 5, 49, 50, 53, 54, 55, 56, 59, 60, 63, 64, 65, 69)

UFO Music Ltd 18 Hanway Street London W1P 9DD England
Telephone: 0171 636 1281   Fax: 0171 636 0738

The author and publishers have made every effort to contact all copyright holders. Any who for any reason have not been contacted are invited to write to the publishers so that a full acknowledgment may be made in subsequent editions of this work.

ISBN 1-873884-94-X

Designed by UFO Music Ltd

Printed by LAWRENCE-ALLEN LTD, Weston-super-Mare

MICHAEL JACKSON

FACTS FROM THE DANCEFLOOR

GEOFF BROWN

MICHAEL JACKSON

King of pop

LONG before he had emerged from his teenage years, Michael Jackson was setting new records, as well as making them, as a phenomenally big-selling pop star. It is very unlikely that the standard he set for commercial appeal and accessibility by selling over 50 million copies of one record alone, *Thriller* will ever be equalled. His four other solo albums recorded as an adult – *Off The Wall*, *Bad*, *Dangerous* and *HIStory* – have sold another 40 million and as a child star fronting the Jackson 5 he was responsible for sales of millions more singles. Today, he is one of the richest men in the world. In the year when allegations of an improper relationship with a minor surfaced, when he did not tour and had no new album out, his earnings amounted to $67m.

His immense wealth has been founded on an outstanding talent for writing and performing pop music. As a child, of course, he had no control over how his talent was used but he learned to sing, record, write and dance so thoroughly and quickly that his mentors, from Tamla Motown boss Berry Gordy to producer Quincy Jones, likened him to a sponge, absorbing information from every possible source. He did this so well that by the time he was old enough to insist on having a greater say in the creation of his own music, Jackson was able to forge a blend of pop, light soul and funk that dominated the airwaves in the early eighties to an unprecedented degree. His big-budget videos and his use of hard rock guitarist Eddie Van Halen (on the *Thriller* track "Beat It") ensured African-American acts at last began to get fairer exposure on MTV.

But in the nineties, the aforementioned charges, a marriage and divorce, a second marriage and the birth of a son, meant that Jackson was in the headlines constantly, but rarely for the excellence of his pop music. Now, he is back where he is most comfortable. On stage, on tour, promoting another album, albeit remixes of his best dance tracks of recent years. Amazingly, he'll be 40 years old next year. He has been singing and dancing for 35 of them.

MICHAEL JACKSON, born August 29, 1958 in Gary, Indiana, had no real chance to grow up "ordinary" because his was not an ordinary childhood. The Jacksons were a large family, ruled by fear by father Joe, a small-time musician. Michael's three elder brothers, Jackie (born Sigmund Esco Jackson on May 4, 1951), Tito (Toriano Adaryll Jackson, born on October 15, 1953) and Jermaine (Jermaine Lajaun Jackson, born December 11, 1954), formed a trio in 1961. Michael, the fifth-born brother, joined a few years later with Marlon David Jackson (born March 12, 1957). Michael's exuberant singing and enthusiastic dancing pushed him out front, and when the commercial ball started rolling in 1969 he was 11 years old and had been fronting the group for six years.

The careers of child stars are traditionally short lived and by all normal criteria Michael's career should have ended 20 years ago as a washed up 19-year-old. But, tyrant though his father might have been, he worked the family hard. "We used to rehearse all the time in Gary," Michael remembered. "Every day when we came home from school. My father made us keep going and put it in our heads that practice makes perfect." The sessions often lasted seven hours but they paid off as the group gradually built a solid reputation as a young act to watch in and round Gary. Michael had no explanation for his talent. "I'd just sing and it came out sounding nice to me." It came out sounding nice to the executives of Motown Records, too.

The Jackson 5 had been playing live since 1965, had won talent contests and in 1967 played at the Apollo Theatre in Harlem, New York. So they were not entirely unknown outside a small area on the Illinois/Indiana borders and had travelled to Philadelphia, Kansas City and St Louis to support name acts. They recorded a few singles for the Michigan label Steeltown – the 1968 ballad "Big Boy" coupled with "You've Changed" was the first – but by the end of the year they'd been signed by Motown.

"One day Gladys Knight told a guy named Bobby Taylor (leader of the Vancouvers) at Motown about us and Motown got hold of us," recalled Michael. Gladys Knight recalls it only slightly differently. "Joe (Jackson, the father) used to come around and talk to me and (the Pips' manager) Taylor Cox. One night they had a talent show at the Regal Theatre and I told Joe we were going to get somebody out there to see them. So they went on and everybody loved them and the next thing I know, big headlines, Diana Ross discovers the Jackson 5! Great, that's all well and good, as long as they were discovered."

Bobby Taylor and Knight had both seen the act and it just so happened that Berry Gordy, who had started Motown Records in the late fifties, was desperate for new, young talent because the established acts on his label – Diana Ross and the Supremes, the Four Tops, Marvin Gaye, Stevie Wonder, the Temptations, Smokey

Robinson and the Miracles – were losing their teen appeal and moving into cabaret and an older market as their fans grew old with them. The Sound Of Young America, as Motown styled itself, didn't sound so young anymore.

So personal recommendation, a home movie and an audition at Berry Gordy's spread won them a contract with Tamla Motown. At the time, the label was in the process of quitting Detroit in the wake of some vicious race riots for the balmy climate of Los Angeles, a move which would not harm Berry Gordy's ambition to produce movies. So the Jackson 5 soon relocated to LA, at first living as house guests in the sumptuous homes of Berry Gordy and his hottest property Diana Ross. It was at the audition in Gordy's home in Detroit that Ross first met Michael and his brothers. "She came over and kissed us and said we were going a long, long way and that she wanted to be part of it."

The signing of the Jackson 5 re-established the company as The Sound Of Young America, shooting it back to the top of the singles' charts four times in 11 months as their new signings became the first new group to hit No 1 with its first four singles. Motown took over the grooming of the Jackson 5's act. The dance and deportment professionals who had tutored the label's long-established stars – the Supremes, the Temptations, the Miracles, the Four Tops – now had a whole new group to work with. Young Motown staffer, Suzanne de Passe, more attuned to their potential audience, coached the boys and took special trouble to tone down some of Michael's more obvious influences – such as James Brown's dance steps. "I'd be in the wings when I was six or seven. I'd sit there and watch him. He's the most electrifying," Michael said of James Brown.

The Jackson 5, like a growing number of popular African-American acts in the late sixties, played their own instruments as well the singing and dancing which was the common currency of the traditional Motown act. But they had not yet started to write their own material. Gordy, who began as a songwriter for Jackie Wilson ("Reet Petite", "To Be Loved", "Lonely Teardrops", "That's Why (I Love You So)", "I'll Be Satisfied" were all US Top 20 hits), well knew the importance of good, original material and the earning power of song-publishing. He had developed the songwriting team Holland-Dozier-Holland and nurtured writers like Smokey Robinson with as much attention as he bestowed on his performers. He put together a writing and production team, The Corporation, which basically comprised himself, Freddie Perren, Alphonso "Fonce" Mizell and Deke Richard,s with occasional help from Bobby Taylor and Hal Davis. They wrote "I Want You Back", the Jacksons' first single released in October, 1969. "I decided I would pattern (Michael's) style after Frankie Lymon," said Gordy. (With his group the Teenagers, Lymon had a Number 1 hit with "Why Do Fools Fall In Love?" in 1956.) "I came up with the melody for the first song we released on the Jackson 5 myself. The kid inspired me so much." By the end of January, 1970 it was No 1 in the United States, selling two million copies. In the UK pop charts it reached No 2.

An album rushed out to cash in on this explosion of popularity used a wide spread of material from standards, Walt Disney, Motown classics and new pop-funk and although there is some filler material it's a zesty LP that succeeded because it concentrated on the group's youthful spirit and natural exuberance, especially

Michael's. "Motown producers didn't let you sing freely," he later recalled, "they told you what to sing. When we started that was fine. But later on…"

To officially launch the group nationally, Motown used The Hollywood Palace Special, an ABC-TV show hosted by Diana Ross and the Supremes although the Jackson 5 had already appeared on The Ed Sullivan, Johnny Carson and the Soul Train US TV shows, three programmes handpicked to give the most comprehensive coverage of the 1969 American singles-buying market.

Jermaine Jackson was the Jackson 5's pin-up and received a large share of fan mail. He was at the right age to win young girls' hearts. But by 1972, at the latest, it had become clear that Michael had the greater all-round talent and, in particular, the better voice. His had a greater range and he had better control, his pitch was sure, his singing was more expressive, he learned quickly and had a voracious appetite for work. In his biography Moonwalk, he said that in 1972, when he was 14, around the time he was recording the "Lookin' Through The Windows" album, he began to challenge the producers' assertions that certain songs should be sung in a certain way. He wrote that he thought Gordy told the producers to give him greater latitude. "I hate everyday love songs. I'm interested in a different type of love song. I want a brand new thought. That's what I loved about "Ben". There's a mystery to it."

Around now, Michael had a growing spurt, as teenagers do, and the cheery-faced boy who twinkled as though about to do something naughty turned into a tall, lean teenager with a case of acne, depressing when you're a kid on the block but deeply worrying when you're centre-stage in the teen sensation act of the decade. The ebullient and confident 12-year-old became a shy and embarrassed 14-year-old. By then, as well as the group's hits, Michael's solo recording career had started. This effectively comprised four albums – *Got To Be There*, *Ben*, *Music & Me* and *Forever Michael*. While *Ben* reached No 5 in the pop album charts there is a sense of similarity throughout the first three solo albums as though they were recorded at one marathon session to get as much material recorded before Michael's young voice changed.

"I Want You Back", the Jackson 5's first hit, was followed quickly in 1970 by "ABC" and "The Love You Save" off their second album (*ABC*). They had sold 10 million singles in nine months. Their third album, deceptively titled *Third Album*, was released in September, 1970 and the first single off it was the Jackson 5's first attempt at a maturer reading of a ballad – "I'll Be There". Ostensibly something of a risk for a

teenage band, it sold two million in the first three days of release. By now, there had sprung up a small industry devoted to new young teenage acts, notably the Osmonds and David Cassidy, late of the Partridge Family, swinging in the coat-tails of the Jackson 5 sound. "I feel (imitation) is a compliment in one way, and in another way you'd be kinda angry. We were the first young group out there with that style, making hit records. There was nobody out there our age... then all of a sudden along came the Osmonds, the Partridge Family. Now you have groups like the Sylvers." the Sylvers, in fact. were produced by Freddie Perren, one of the then-disbanded Corporation writing/production team.

As noted earlier, Michael had started to voice reservations about the way in which Motown was recording the group – and the material it was being presented with – as early as 1972's *Lookin' Through The Windows* album. In 1973, with the group's "Skywriter" album in the stores, Berry Gordy registered the name the Jackson 5 as Motown's property, which would later prove to be a very contentious move. The title track of 1973's *Get It Together* found Michael almost overnight sounding like a young adult rather than the piping teenager and the album's last track, "Dancing Machine", provided the group with a very unexpected Top 10 hit (since 1971's "Never Can Say Goodbye" had reached Number 2, no Jackson 5 single had made it into the US Top 10) thanks to the disco boom.

By 1975, the Jackson 5's creative impasse at Motown was complete. Jermaine, who had recorded several solo albums for Motown and become "romantically involved", as the American gossip magazines of the day would have put it, with Hazel Gordy, Berry's daughter, was literally wedded to the label. But the remaining brothers were determined to get into a situation where they could exercise more control over their music and to move in a more mature direction. Michael's voice had manifestly changed. The old style and content would no longer do.

The solo album *Forever Michael* paralleled the Jackson 5's *Moving Violation* LP which was released at roughly the same time. At the time neither was praised but there is a clear evidence of further maturity and a pointer to the group's and Michael's future. The dance tracks are more robust and Jackson's lead vocals now sound like those of a young adult rather than a growing kid. The tracks on *Forever Michael* produced by Brian Holland, co-writer Eddie Holland and Michael are promising enough for the team to have been given a whole album but Jackson had tired of

Motown's production treadmill, had learnt all that they had to teach and wanted to write and produce his own material.

By now, the stage shows had evolved from the screaming, teenybop concert tours to more "adult" venues. In the spring of 1974, the entire clan of Jackson siblings – the brothers Michael, Jermaine, Jackie, Tito and Marlon plus the youngest boy, Randy, and sisters Maureen ("Rebbie"), Janet and LaToya – unveiled their new cabaret act at the start of a season performing at the MGM Grand Hotel in Las Vegas. An attempt to cast aside their teenybop image in the traditional Motown way, by "going Vegas".

Diversifying the attention from Michael would have been a better way, perhaps, but in the talent stakes, the cards had not been dealt evenly among the Jacksons. While they had been at Motown, Michael was not the only brother to release solo albums. As soon as his solo career had been successfully launched plans were laid for the four other brothers to be similarly launched as solo stars, generating another four new sources of income to the group and Michael's and, it was hoped, making them less reliant on Michael as the main breadwinner. Nice strategy but, alas, only one other Jackson brother had success as a solo artist. Marlon did not record as a solo act until long after the split with Motown and although plans for a predominantly instrumental album by guitarist Tito were laid, no-one seemed in much of a rush to pick them up. *Jackie Jackson*, the eldest brother's eponymous first effort, was a soft-edged, sweet-toned album released in January, 1974 in the UK to general disinterest leaving Jermaine, the original pin-up of the group, as the only Jackson to record with any frequency and achieve a hit or two.

His first album, *Jermaine*, was released in January, 1973, a month after Michael's "Ben", but it sold well enough, helped by "Daddy's Home", a cover of Shep and the Limelites' 1961 hit. In America, the ballad reached No 9 in the pop singles chart. The treatment was just-right for Jermaine's more vulnerable-sounding voice, which did not have the strength or emotional expression of Michael's. Jermaine's second album, *Come Into My Life*, (September, 1973) was released two month's after Michael's *Music And Me*. Because of the success of "Daddy's Home" there was greater emphasis put on ballads, which he and Motown quickly realised were his best style.

By the time Jermaine's next album, *My Name Is Jermaine*, was released in October, 1976, he was the sole Jackson at Motown. He married Hazel, Berry Gordy's daughter, on December 15, 1974 and remained loyal to his father-in-law when the other five Jacksons – youngest brother Randy (Steven Randall Jackson) had now joined the ranks – lived up to their promise, as announced first on June 30, 1975, to break away from Motown and sign with a company which would afford them more, if not absolute, creative control and to let them, Michael especially, become more involved in writing, arrangement and production. Surely Motown saw this coming? In the recording studio he had the reputation of being "a sponge" soaking up tips, tricks-of-the-trade, whatever useful information there was to be had. Those many hours he spent at the rehearsal rooms, at the piano in the recording studio, all the techniques he'd painstakingly acquired, created a deep well of ambition. Motown chose not to dip into it.

In *Moonwalk*, Michael says he was the only brother with the courage to go head-to-head with Berry Gordy and demand more control over their career. (Marvin Gaye and Stevie Wonder, longer-serving Motown artists, had famously battled for the same earlier in the seventies and had provided the label with classic albums as a result: Gaye's *What's Going On* and *Let's Get It On*; Wonder's *Talking Book*, *Innervisions* and *Fullfillingness' First Finale*). Jermaine, who remained at Motown, told a different story. Successful in 1979 with *Let's Get Serious*, he insisted that, "It wasn't my decision to be solo. This is not what I wanted to do. But I had no choice…Usually when you hear of somebody going someplace else at least you would sit down and have a discussion about it. The first thing I saw was all the contracts with their names on it, so they had already left. They figured by signing ahead of time, I would go ahead and sign." Jermaine insisted that Michael "never wanted to leave. Because he was too young to voice a strong opinion, to say 'No father, I am not going, I am very happy where I am.'"

Had the group panicked when the hits stopped up after their extraordinary launch? "All of a sudden, that cools off one would probably get nervous and say, 'Well, what's wrong?'" The easy option, and it might have been the correct one, was to blame the record company. "But everybody, they're hot for a while and then they cool off. As big as the Beatles were, they cooled off and split up and had individual success."

But Michael's words are the bottom line. "Motown producers didn't let you sing freely, they told you what to sing. When we started that was fine, but later on…" Not that the producers were unsympathetic. Freddie Perren, once part of The Corporation team, with the benefit of hindsight, said, "There is a certain talent that

goes with songwriting and I could see that he had it. Motown just didn't encourage it in performers. At Motown the producer was king."

And so the Jacksons quit Motown and signed to CBS who put them on the Epic label. Renamed the Jacksons after discovering Gordy's aforementioned business manoeuvre of registering the Jackson 5 name as the property of Motown, the five brothers, with Randy in as permanent replacement for Jermaine, were placed with producers Kenny Gamble and Leon Huff, the founders of Philadelphia International Records, who had created the Philly Sound that had grabbed a sizable share of the soul market in the seventies. Just as Motown's hit factory in Detroit had been the blueprint for urban soul in the sixties, so the sophisticated sounds atop a strong dance beat that poured out of the Sigma Sound Studios in Philadelphia typified a particular kind of uptown seventies soul. Gamble and Huff made hit singles but their artists' albums sold well too – the O'Jays, Harold Melvin and the Blue Notes featuring Teddy Pendergrass and the Intruders were three of the groups benefiting – and the lyric ideas often had more adult themes which the Jacksons could certainly use. The Jackson 5 had covered many Philly songs on their Motown albums, songs which had been hits for the Stylistics and the Delfonics among others. These were a more sugary kind of Philly; whereas Kenny Gamble and Leon Huff got down with a slightly harder style, often favouring singers like Pendergrass and the O'Jays' Eddie Levert who could display a sweaty passion. Teenybop, it was not. But would it work for The Jacksons?

"We had a lot of fun working with them," said Leon Huff. "What we were trying to do was to broaden their audience. They were in a natural period of transition that reflected their growth… It sounded good to us. We had them all singing, that was new." Huff said that the experience the Jacksons gained in the studio with them helped the group towards being able to produce themselves.

The Epic debut, *The Jacksons*, released in the USA in November, 1976, had been preceded by two Motown compilations: *The Jackson 5 Anthology* and *Joyful Jukebox Music*. As a tactic designed to do material damage to the Jacksons' new-label launch, it was not entirely successful. Although *Anthology* was worthwhile, the wretched *Joyful Jukebox Music* was the first Jackson 5 album to miss the Top 200 US albums charts.

At Sigma, Michael absorbed all the songwriting advice and production tips that Gamble and Huff had to offer, particularly the construction of a song because the group was now penning material they hoped to get on the album. Compared to the last

few Jackson 5 albums, *The Jacksons* was a significant advance. The balance of tracks on the album was fairly typical of all Gamble and Huff productions: mixing Philly dance tracks, love songs and songs which voiced concerns about the moral and physical future of mankind and the planet, it set the controls for the next period of their career. Side one of the album – "Enjoy Yourself", "Think Happy", "Good Times", "Keep On Dancing" and "Blues Away" - exuded a very positive, sunny vibe; so much so that it is difficult to visualise a rosier mood.

The tone and range of Michael's voice had changed and the producers allowed him greater freedom to interpret their melody and words. It is very apparent, too, that without anyone sufficiently gifted to share lead vocals as Jermaine had once done, Jackie, Marlon, Tito and Randy would continue to provide vocal harmonies and background but the Jacksons had effectively become The Michael Jackson Group.

Motown had launched the Jackson 5 in America with four straight No 1 hits. But they'd never topped the charts in Britain. Yet "Show You The Way To Go", the second single off *The Jacksons*, gave the family its first British No 1 hit, seven years after the UK release of "I Want You Back". *Goin' Places*, the second Gamble and Huff-produced Jacksons album on Epic, was largely an expansion on the style they had established on *The Jacksons*. Released in October, 1976 it was another feelgood collection with Gamble and Huff stoking up the Love Train.

While the Jacksons' recording and touring had been going on, Michael was involved in a side project – his movie acting debut. *The Wiz*, a rewriting of *The Wizard Of Oz* as an all-black stage musical, had been a Broadway smash and Diana

Ross coveted the lead role of Dorothy. After impressing many observers with her performance as Billie Holiday in *Lady Sings The Blues*, Ross' screen career had stalled with the disastrous *Mahogany*. And now, despite being manifestly too old for the role, she used her influence to grab the part. Michael Jackson was cast as the Scarecrow, one of the three companions who travel with Dorothy down the yellow brick road to find the Wizard of Oz and the answers to their prayers. Michael's all-singing, all-dancing role featured an excellent performance of "You Can't Win", which was a bright moment in a fairly cheerless movie. More important than any of this, however, was the meeting on the project between Michael and Quincy Jones. "His performance in *The Wiz* is just mind-boggling," said Jones, "even for an old-timer, let alone someone who's taking his first shot at film" Jones thought that because the first time he worked with Michael was as an actor, rather than the teenybop star he'd always imagined him as, he was able to get a different perspective on Jackson's maturing talent. "I started to see this disciplined curious mind. He'd come in at five o'clock to do make-up and they'd start shooting at seven. He knew everybody's lines, every part, he never complained."

Some while after filming had finished, Jackson decided to resume his solo recording career – Motown hadn't registered his name as their property – and rang Jones to ask his advice on who he should hire as producer. In the end, Michael asked Quincy to go into the studio with him. It was to be the most significant working partnership in Michael's career, bar none.

But first, there was the small matter of the third Jacksons' album. It was an auspicious moment. Epic assigned Bobby Colomby, the former Blood Sweat and Tears drummer, and Mike Atkinson as executive producers but it was a Jacksons-production and the group was writing a lot of material. The aptly-named *Destiny*, released in December, 1978, was the first recording for Peacock Productions, a newly-formed company which the Jacksons had named for the bird whose lustrous plumage "integrates all colours into one, and displays this radiance of fire only when in love". Ahem. Immodestly, they likened themselves to the peacock integrating the entire human race through a love of music.

Thumping dance tracks like "Blame It On The Boogie", "Shake Your Body (Down To The Ground)", "All Night Dancer" and "Things I Do For You" interspersed with wistful ballads of unfulfilled love in "Push Me Away" and "That's What You Get (For Being Polite)" pulled together as complete an album as they'd yet

DESTINY

made. "*Destiny* was the beginning of the whole thing and the timing was so right," he recalled. It "broke the ice for us as producers, too. It provided a direction for the future." Michael, still not out of his teens, teased by his less talented brothers who, he said in his book Moonwalk, called him "Big Nose", was now even more important to the family business. He was now the group's meal ticket. A good time, then, to pick up the solo career which had lain dormant since the label switch in 1975.

During the writing and recording of *Destiny*, Michael started to hold back ideas for songs that he thought would make better tracks for a solo album. He was growing more miserable in the group context, the need to find space for the four brothers, but the tour to support *Destiny* emphasised his new-found broad appeal. It was now that he broke off from his his sole management contract with Joe Jackson, his father, when it expired in 1979 making him joint-manager with Freddie DeMann and Ron Weisner of the mainstream firm Weisner-DeMann Entertainment. And the aforementioned conversation with Quincy Jones about who'd make a good producer for a modern solo album ended when Jones agreed to take on the job. "Quincy does jazz, movie scores, rock'n'roll, funk, pop – he's all colours and that's the kind of people I like to work with." The partnership's successes are well known. With a tight team of musicians and the engineer Bruce Swedien, they broke almost every sales record that existed, created a few more of their own and installed Jackson as the recording phenomenon of his generation. Throughout the eighties, Michael's vocal trademarks would be copied by other pop vocalists and the style of the tracks became a template for eighties pop.

Plans to name the set "Girlfriend" after a song Paul McCartney gave to Michael before the Jones/Jackson project got under way had to be scrapped when the former Beatle guessed that Michael didn't want the song and added "Girlfriend" to his own *London Town* LP. Nonetheless, Michael recorded the song, adding it to nine others, including three by the hit writer and keyboard player out of Heatwave, Rod Temperton. "I still feel that I'm really not and never was a songwriter. When George Gershwin and those kind of people were around, they wrote songs. They wrote on a piano, there was a melody, chords and it stood up on its own. Today, we're writing records not songs. You've got to know how to make a record. And so that's what I do. I write to go on tape and the song is never usually finished until the day it goes in the shop." One of Temperton's songs that aren't songs, *Off The Wall*, became the new title track of the 10-song album, five of which would become hit singles in their own right.

Released in August, 1979, *Off The Wall*, although not his biggest-selling album, is regarded by many to be his best album, a landmark black pop-soul record. "When Quincy and I first started we sat down and discussed exactly what we wanted and it has all turned out the way we planned... but if anything it has done more than we expected. We aimed for triple platinum and now it's on its way to five million." Sales went way past that figure: worldwide it sold 12 million copies. In Britain it was the first album from which five hit singles were lifted and it was on the UK charts for 173 weeks. It's hard to find fault with the quite magical mixture of nimble dance tracks, bubbly love songs and ballads and the blend of styles skipping from pop and disco to soul and light funk.

Thirteen months after *Off The Wall*, the Jacksons were back in business with the release of *Triumph*, the last good album the group would cut. Michael dominates it to an even greater extent than he had controlled the tone and direction of *Destiny*. But, cannily, he also gives away less of the vocal eccentricities on *Triumph*, holding those catches of breath, squeals and other exclamations for his solo work. Once again the Jacksons wrote and produced everything, with an audible shift from the "band" feel of *Destiny* towards bigger productions and arrangements. Just as at Motown the launch of Michael's solo career foreshadowed the decline of the Jackson 5, now Michael's return to solo recording had hinted that the Jacksons' prosperity as a group was about to be materially affected. Sales of *Triumph*, though respectable, were dwarfed by *Off The Wall*. And, for them, worse was to come.

But what of Jermaine, the brother left behind at Motown? His first album after the split seemed to recognise the need to stamp his identity. *My Name Is Jermaine* was a tentative start, working through influences to find his style and voice post-5. The next album, in September, 1977, was *Feel The Fire*. Jermaine co-wrote three of the nine tracks with co-producer Michael McGloiry and he wrote "Got To Get You Girl" alone. He was also writing for the new Motown signings Switch, another family group (the DeBarges) he had discovered. Jermaine and McGloiry worked on four of the nine tracks on *Frontiers*, (April, 1978). But his most successful solo album, artistically and commercially, was *Let's Get Serious* (April, 1980). Three out of its seven tracks were co-produced by Jermaine and Stevie Wonder, who also contributed keyboards, guitar,

drums and synthesiser. The Wonder/Lee Garrett-penned title track remains Jermaine's most likable solo track.

The success of *Serious* was all-too-quickly followed by another solo album, *Jermaine*, released at the end of 1980. By now he was writing almost all of his own material but his time was running out at Motown. *I Like Your Style* (October, 1981) and *Let Me Tickle Your Fancy* (August, 1982), brought the curtain down on his Motown stage of his career. In the intervening years he'd turned into a useful producer and as a singer showed a preference for ballads, while even the dancefloor tracks were performed and produced in a sort of aural soft focus.

Several tracks on his last three albums for the label were bursting with heavy hints that he'd like to get back with his brothers. The likelihood of a reunited "Jackson 6" was increased by the guest appearances by Tito and Randy, the brother who had replaced him in the family act, on *Let Me Tickle Your Fancy*. Some time later, Jermaine decided that his future lay outside Motown. There were people at Motown, he said, adding that he was not referring to Berry Gordy, with whom he could no longer work. He left Motown in 1983 and signed to Arista.

If it were at all possible, the booming sales of and critical acclaim lavished on *Off The Wall* raised Michael's profile even higher. His peers in the music industry were very happy to have him guest on their tracks and in the years 1980-82 he did sessions with Quincy Jones, Diana Ross (he wrote and produced "Muscles"; a track sharing the name of his pet snake, for her *Silk Electric* album), Stevie Wonder, Brothers Johnson, Donna Summer, Minnie Riperton, sister LaToya Jackson (producing and co-writing "Night Time Lover"), Kenny Loggins (formerly of Loggins & Messina), Dave Mason (once a member of Traffic), crossover country star Kenny Rogers, songwriter Carole Bayer Sager and one Joe "King" Carrasco. In that period, of course, he also returned to the Jacksons, with less than 100 per cent willingness, to record *Triumph*, the follow-up to *Destiny*. With such a workaholic schedule and after the esteem of his peers there followed, as sure as night follows day, heightened media interest. People began to take notice of the changing face of Michael Jackson, the gradual appearance of a thinner, more sculpted nose, a cleft in his chin, a lighter skin tone (brought on, he says, by an illness which affects the skin's pigmentation).

No amount of absorbing information like a sponge could ever make Jackson better at coping with the media. He could exercise little control over what the

press wrote about him, he slowly realised, and in the eighties made himself largely unavailable for interviews. He'd never enjoyed that sort of direct spotlight. At one stage, when he was persuaded to do press interviews for the promotion of an album or tour, he insisted that the questions were put to his sister Janet, who would then whisper them into his ear, receive the answer and, like a translator, relay them back to the interviewer. Much further down the line, he would use appearances on selected TV shows, notably an appearance on the *Oprah Winfrey show* in 1993, to refute the media's image of him as a crazy and dangerous manchild.

By then, of course, he had asserted his mission to live in a world where there would be no hunger, where peace would reign and suffering be banished, sentiments one could scarcely argue with. "I believe I can help achieve that goal if I stay healthy in mind and body. I believe that if I live correctly I can live to be 150." Statements like that tended to reinforce the belief that Michael was indeed off the wall. "My biggest fear is being misquoted... Lately, people have been twisting everything I've been saying and that's why I shy away from interviews. I don't like to be misrepresented to my fans." Rumours, he added, he couldn't stop but misquotations were serious. "If I can't be quoted properly, I'd rather not be quoted at all." So he stopped doing interviews altogether.

Thus the media was forced to feed his fans' passion for information by focusing on Michael's "abnormal" lifestyle and the veritable menagerie that shared his home. In addition to Muscles, a boa constrictor, Louis the Llamas, Bubbles the chimp, Mr Tibbs the sheep, and Prince and Princess, a pair of fawns, he owned many birds; creating the first tier in Michael's reputation as a rich young man with the wealth to indulge some fairly eccentric tastes. One fact is noteworthy: much of what he says he likes is attributed to its quality of "escapism". Dance (be it a night at the Studio 54 nightclub or his Sunday ritual – no food, just vegetable juice to cleanse the system, a day devoted to dancing) or his apparently endless fascination with Disneyland or his affection for the film ET, the classic MGM and Disney cartoons, comedies by the Three Stooges or just performing on stage. That, he has said famously, is the only place where he feels safe and at home. "I'd sleep on stage if I could. My whole life has been on stage and the impression I get of people is applause, standing ovations and running after you." Control of the situation, safety and a joyful energy exploding from within are his most general impressions of being on stage.

Contrasting with the young, fairly hard-nosed businessman who was able take tough decisions, not the least of which was to sack his father as sole manager, came a parallel image of a shy young man, awkward with adults, still child-like in some ways when it came to social intercourse. "I do feel strange with people," he once said. "All my life I've been treated differently from other people. It does make you shy." His girlfriends – Tatum O'Neal, Brooke Shields – had been child star actresses and he later forged friendships with women he'd seen and admired in movies or on stage, notably Elizabeth Taylor but also Katharine Hepburn, Jane Fonda, Liza Minelli and, of course, his "mother-lover-friend" Diana Ross. Outside of the music business, adult male friends seemed very thin on the ground.

Even cloistered in the grounds of the Jackson family home in Los Angeles, California, he could not feel entirely safe. When the family first moved there from Gary, Indiana, the Jacksons' house was quickly added to the tourist map of stars' homes which can be bought on many street corners or from vendors at the side of the road. The home was inundated. One morning, Michael awoke to find a girl, a complete stranger, standing beside his bed. Fans would be found sleeping in the grounds. They quickly had Hollywood-style security installed. When he ventured outside the family fortress in Encino, he put on disguises to hide from both press and fans. Presumably they worked, but often when snapped by the paparazzi his disguise would look more like a costume yelling, Look at me! Look at me!

Back at his career, the National Academy of Recording Arts And Sciences (NARAS) had ignored *Off The Wall* in the Grammy nominations and although the track "Don't Stop 'Til You Get Enough" won one it was a slap in the face because, clearly, it was an outstanding record of the time, one of the biggest sellers of the year and as time went by was proving to be hugely influential. Also, it had been snubbed by MTV, which at the time operated an unspoken policy of musical apartheid – no soul, no R&B, in other words, no African-Americans.

Jackson was determined to better *Off The Wall* and set to work with Quincy Jones, re-hiring roughly the same team, but using guest musicians with a rock-orientated background to give the music a greater focus on the white market. Using another three songs from Rod Temperton, including the title track which picked up Michael's fascination with horror movies and included narration by Vincent Price, the Hammer horror veteran, the singer himself wrote another four of the nine tracks, all of them about confrontation in varying degrees of seriousness. His singing was now distinctive as never before, full of expressive catches and clicks, whoops and squeals. Jackson's rampaging dance track, "Wanna Be Startin' Somethin'", written when *Off The Wall* was being recorded, got the whole thing off to a thundering start and the lyrics to two other uptempo dance tracks, "Beat It" and "Billie Jean", were spat out with something approaching anger. Again, there was a duet with Paul McCartney, the rather gentle squabble "The Girl Is Mine", and a couple of indelibly catchy pop-soul ballads, notably "Human Nature" and Temperton's "Baby Be Mine".

Released in December, 1982 the album, *Thriller*, became the listening accessory everyone had to have. Seven of the nine tracks were hit singles, each one generating more album sales. To promote the singles, Jackson spent time and a lot of money on high production values videos, Michael eventually breaking through MTV's racial barrier. His appearance on the *Motown 25: Yesterday, Today, Forever* NBC-TV special, when an estimated 47 million viewers saw him perform the Moonwalk dance, gave the album's sales yet another thrust. By the summer of 1983, *Thriller* had sold seven million of them in the USA, 10 million copies worldwide. To an industry in the

throes of a recession the album's phenomenal success was a godsend because by attracting shoppers into record stores it was helping the waning sales of other acts.

It's said that the truly rich man does not know how much money he's worth and the same could be said for the sales of *Thriller*, 52 million copies at the lower end of the scale, 54 at the top. And he wreaked revenge of the Grammy Awards, walking off with Album of the Year, Record of the Year (for "Beat It"), Best Pop Vocal Performance, Male, Best Rock Vocal Performance, Male (for "Beat It"), Best New Rhythm & Blues Song and Best R&B Vocal Performance, Male (both for "Billie Jean") and Best Recording For Children (for narration and vocals on "E.T. The Extra-Terrestrial", based on the Steven Spielberg movie – "Of all the awards I've got, I'm most proud of this one," he said). The Grammy for Best Engineered Recording (Non-Classical) went to *Thriller* engineer Bruce Swedien and Quincy Jones, and Jackson picked up Producer Of The Year (Non-Classical). Sixty million Americans watched the Grammy Awards on TV and in the seven days following the broadcast "Thriller" sold another million copies in the US alone. (1798)

With such a long-selling album, Michael's brothers could expect no great enthusiasm from their sibling for starting up the Jacksons' career again while, from their point of view, it is impossible to believe that there was not an amount of envy at the way his solo career had mushroomed as his contribution to the group's output fell and their star dimmed. But in 1984 there was an album, tour and multi-million dollar deal with Pepsi Cola which ought to have placated them somewhat. As ever, the best laid plans…

While filming a commercial as part of the Pepsi Cola deal, Michael's hair was set alight when one of the flashes ignited gel on his follicles. He was rushed to hospital and though not life-threatening the burns he suffered left his hairline considerably damaged. He recorded his fifth studio album as the Jacksons for Epic with his brothers – there had been a "Live" album released in 1981 – and unwillingly embarked on a 55-date tour to promote the Jacksons' album, *Victory*, which did little to enhance the reputations of the participants by attracting paragraphs of negative publicity over the price of the tickets, the exorbitant marketing deals, the overall greed, the lack of African-American promoters used.

The problem which loomed was that *Victory* needed all the live show support it could get, because by once again trying to sell the Jacksons as a "democratic" group enjoying equal share of the limelight and the creative burden as singers, writers or producers, it had totally misread the audiences' perception. "Michael's got a good show," his father memorably said, "but with the brothers it's a better show." By relegating The King Of Pop to a player in an ensemble – there were only two Michael Jackson songs on *Victory*, neither of which would have made it on to *Off The Wall* or *Thriller* – the Jackson threw away their ace. Still, the tour would reunite Jermaine with his brothers on stage although they'd made a one-off appearance at the Motown 25th Anniversary show. "It was very emotional for me," Jermaine said, "the whole evening was emotional for us all. It really felt like being home again." Another, bigger bonus was the fact that Michael had not toured in support of, or since, *Thriller*. This meant that the *Victory* stadium tour was always going to be one of the hottest tickets around. Until, that was, the ticketing prices and arrangements were announced.

Even the increasing publicity about Michael's hobbies and press perception of him as slightly wacky could not have prepared him for the backlash which surrounded the "Victory" tour, even before a note had been played. There was continual sniping between promoters and management which at one point forced him to apologise for the alleged racist remarks by his father, Joe Jackson. Frank DiLeo, the vice-president of promotions at Epic who had been in charge of the impressive marketing campaign for "Thriller", was appointed personal manager by Michael. Joe Jackson had become allied with Don King, the boxing promoter, and the brothers were signed for management to Frank Nance, a former Jackson 5 tour manager.

Several promoters put in bids for the stadium tour but in the end Chuck

Sullivan won. He knew all about stadia through his involvement with the New England Patriots American Football team but had next to no knowledge of pop concert promotion. He pledged that the Jacksons would earn $40m from the tour. Ticket prices for the tour were set at $28 plus a $2 handling fee, the tickets to be available by mail only and in blocks of four. Thus the outlay would be $120.

Even this did not assure the fans of a ticket. The lucky ones would be drawn from a lottery; the rest would get their money back – after it had been earning interest in the promoters' account. So not only was the tab, in 1984, way outside the pockets of most young African-American fans, a market which in any case is traditionally known as one which tends to buy tickets on the night, not in advance, there was no guarantee that the outlay would buy a ticket. A not uncommon method of ticket dispersal in Britain, it was considered a mighty scam in the USA and was abandoned shortly before the start of the tour when Michael acted. "The other day I got a letter from a girl in Texas named Ladonnia Jones," he said via a prepared statement. "She'd been saving her money from odd jobs to buy a ticket, but with the current tour system she'd have to buy four tickets and she couldn't afford that. So I've asked our promoter to work out a new way of distributing tickets – a way that no longer requires a $120 money order. I've asked our promoter to end the mail order system as soon as possible so that no one will pay money unless they get a ticket." At the same time, Jackson announced that he would donate his personal earnings from the 13-city 30-show tour to charities.

Democracy may have reigned when it came to recording "Victory" and the division of the spoils of the tour but when it came to "Showtime!" the focus was on Michael, apart from a 15-minute interlude when the focus shifted to Jermaine. The tour was not a success. Sniping and dissension continued for most of the tour and the hapless promoter, Chuck Sullivan, ended up in hospital before the end, having suffered a heart attack. His estimated loss on the tour was $18m. "It's been a long 20 years," Michael said at the end of the tour. "This is our final farewell tour as a family."

Jermaine and the rest of the brothers blamed the managers and promoters. "The only fights we had were with the promoters," said Jermaine. "All that publicity was people making up juicy stories for entertainment. I'm afraid that's the kind of business I'm in." The promoters, said eldest brother Jackie, "want to be stars themselves… it's like power games they're playing. I know it. We all know it. They must know it." Tito's response was all that could be expected from a member of the tight Jackson unit. "It's always the outside people who cause the problems."

Everyone wants to do better than they did before. Alas, when an album has sold well over 50 million copies and the singles from it have dominated the charts and airwaves there is bound to be a little weariness in that part of the audience which are not core, diehard fans. Thus when, in the run-up to the September, 1987 release of the follow-up to *Thriller*, Michael was confidently predicting that sales would outstrip those of the biggest-selling album of all time, one could sense that his ambition and expectations had been raised to an unrealistically high level. Much better to simply make an album for oneself and hope for the best because in pop music, who says biggest sales mean the best? Was *Thriller* that much better than *Off The Wall* if it was better at all?

The fiasco of 1984's *Victory* tour, and a stream of tales about his business arrangements and rumours concerning his private life, built a picture of a Peter Pan-like creature with, more disposable income than he knew what to do with making smart business deals – paying $47.5m to acquire the ATV publishing catalogue which included the best Beatles' songs – while the tabloids dub him Wacko Jacko as he doorsteps for the Jehovah's Witnesses or allegedly tries to buy the bones of John Merrick, the Elephant Man. With Quincy Jones, Stevie Wonder, Lionel Richie and Dionne Warwick, among others,

he recorded "We Are The World" in aid of African famine relief, and launched a range of stuffed, fluffy animals – Michael's Pets – and he took two-and-a-half years to write and record *Bad*.

Between *Thriller* (1982) and *Bad* (1987) pop music had changed quite radically. African-American music got tougher-sounding because of developments in instrument technology and the harder, streetsier lyrics and rhymes used by the hardcore hip-hop acts. But Michael had assembled approximately the same crew to record his 1987 project. Stickers on *Bad* promised that "The Thrill Is Back!!" and "10 Brand New Hits!!!" Searching for a contemporary sound, the rhythm leaned heavily on synthesisers forcing Jackson to sing in a not always convincing aggressive tone. Many of the songs were forgettable despite a messianic tone to many of the lyrics. He was clearly trying to toughen up his visual image too. Gone was the tuxedo (*Off The Wall*) and white suit (*Thriller*). For *Bad* he belted, buckled and zippered up a "rebel with a cause" black jacket and looked ludicrous: who was he trying to kid?

The pre-release hype on *Bad* worked. One in four albums sold in Britain in the first five days of its release was *Bad* and in the US the album stayed in the Top 5 for 38 weeks. The hype even generated more sales of *Off The Wall* and *Thriller*. He could not be accused of not supporting the album, setting off on a huge world tour and filming big-budget videos. There were four consecutive No 1 hit singles pulled off it – only the soundtrack to *Saturday Night Fever* had achieved that before – which made Michael the first artist to have four consecutive No 1s as a group member and as a solo artist. *Bad* sold 15 million copies worldwide in its first nine months, a not at all poor sales performance with three US No1s – the title track, "Dirty Diana" and "The Way You Make Me Feel" – despite its patchy quality. A part of the reason the album kept selling so well was Michael's spectacular live shows, spiced with his ever-extraordinary dancing and eye-boggling special effects.

To return briefly to the Jacksons, Marlon had left the group after the *Victory* tour. "I went to Epic and told them I wanted to do a solo album, they said they wanted a group album first, that maybe I could do a solo project after we did that, so that's when I decided I should officially leave." He did his solo album, *Baby Tonight*, for Capitol in 1987. Two years after that, the remaining Jacksons – Jackie, Tito, Jermaine and Randall, as Randy was now known – made a Jacksons album without Michael, apart from the smallest possible appearance on the title track along with sister Rebbie's kids

and Marlon. Jermaine dominates *2300 Jackson Street*, singing most leads and co-writes on eight of the 11 tracks. Crucially, the Jacksons recruited several hot producer/writers, notably Teddy Riley and LA Reid & Babyface, who had been pioneering a post-Michael Jackson style of pop-soul, swingbeat. Released in July, 1989, the album's title track gives the address of their old home in Gary, Indiana – the street was eventually named after the group – painting a picture of happy family life which subsequent books, especially those by Michael and sister LaToya, disagree with quite markedly.

Meanwhile, Michael had been on the road forever, promoting *Bad* on a record-breaking world tour which helped the album become the biggest-selling record of 1987. It continued to sell well throughout the following 12 months. Towards the end of the tour he announced that it was to be his last, he published Moonwalk, his autobiographical memoir, and released the video *Moonwalker*, which would sell more than *The Making Of Thriller* and after four frantic years he parted company with manager Frank Dileo. But he still wasn't talking to the press and the barrage of hype around "Bad" created a swell of anti-Jackson feeling in the media. So they began to dig around for more How Wacko Is Jacko? type stories which left readers in no doubt that Michael Jackson equalled odd behaviour.

Work on his fourth Epic solo album began at the end of 1989. After a year, its release was put back to the early summer of 1991, then to late summer and finally to November. He had accumulated some 70 songs from which 14 were chosen. Sony, the Japanese manufacturers which had bought Epic's parent Columbia, signed him to a new 15-year recording and film-making deal which could net him up to a billion dollars in return for six albums at a royalty rate of 25 per cent. He was advanced $18m for the new project.

After three albums Jackson severed the link with producer Quincy Jones, choosing to work with Teddy Riley, the writer/producer who'd defined the new swingbeat with his own three-piece Guy and his work on younger acts. Riley, it will be remembered, had also worked on *2300 Jackson Street*. "He told me I was the best producer out there," said Riley. The difference between Michael and his brothers, he added, was that Michael knew what he wante;, his brothers didn't. "Michael prepares, he practises at home, he sleeps with the tape on. And then, when he gets to the studio he can just knock it out." If Jackson wanted to get back to "blacker" pop-soul sounds,

he'd made an intelligent choice. Seven songs on *Dangerous* were co-written and/or produced with Riley and Jackson produced the remainder with engineer Bruce Swedien or co-writer, Bill Bottrell. The guests included rapper Heavy D, and metal guitarist Slash from Guns N' Rose, signalling the album's mix of hard, synthesised dance sounds, rock songs and softer ballads.

Despite his announcement at the end of the *Bad* tour that he would not be taking to the road again, he toured to promote *Dangerous*. In Britain, *Dangerous* was joined in the Top 50 by his three previous Epic solo albums along with a Special Tour Souvenir Pack, a 12-song, 4-picture CD box set. Sluggish sales homeland were worrying until he arranged appearances on two of the country's high-profile TV shows with huge viewing figures – singing four songs as the half-time entertainment to the 1993 Super Bowl (133 million viewers) and chatting on *The Oprah Winfrey Show* (85 million). As publicity coups go, this was special.

It was the final piece of good news for some while. In August 1993, he was accused of child abuse by the parents of 13-year-old Jordy Schwarz Chandler. Early in the Los Angeles police's investigation, it was alleged that Evan Chandler, Jordy's father, had attempted, without success, to get Michael's backing for a film project and had gone ahead with his threat to "expose" the singer as a child molester. The investigations, claims, counter-claims, and depositions by several of Jackson's former employees all confirming the allegations ran until January 1994 when the LA police stated that they did not have sufficient evidence to charge Evan Chandler with extortion and/or blackmail and, similarly, the evidence against Jackson was poor (Jordy's descriptions of Jackson's genitalia did not match the photographic evidence obtained, humiliatingly according to Michael, by the police). The Chandler vs Jackson case was settled for an undisclosed sum, reportedly £10m ($15m). Jackson never had his day in court to refute the charges but continued to deny them – an appearance to do so on an American TV show in 1995 resulted in further allegations a year later that Jackson and the TV network had set out to "falsely accuse the minor... of lying about his claims".

There is no doubt that the case has had a catastrophic effect on his standing in the USA. Bearing in mind the positive publicity he had gained from his donations to children's charities, his apparent innocent affinity with kids, the charges were ruinous. Businesswise, his long-term advertising contract with Pepsi-Cola was cancelled; he cancelled some concerts but later resumed the world tour, claiming that he had become dependent on painkillers to help him finish the dates. As evidence, he was interviewed in front of a video camera, slurring his words and sounding as blurry as he looked.

Against this sordid background, ran the saga of *HIStory*. A "Greatest Hits" album was first mooted back in 1989, scheduled for November 1993 release with a couple of bonus tracks. Delayed by ongoing uncertainty about the outcome of the child abuse accusations, the deluge of negative publicity and slow progress on new songs, Michael suddenly decided that he would match the "Hits" CD not with a couple of new tracks but with an entire CD of new material.

Oh, and he got married on May 26, 1994. The notion of Michael Jackson, Peter Pan of Pop, marrying at all was risible but that he should marry Lisa Marie Presley, only daughter of Elvis, the late King of Rock'n'Roll, and Priscilla Presley struck many as at best laughable, at worst a cynical ploy to deflect the lingering doubts many people in the USA still had about the accusations levelled against him, primarily by the Chandlers. Lisa Marie had been married before, to musician Danny Keough, and had two children. She divorced Keough three weeks before marrying Jackson in the Dominican Republic, and they later went on American TV to deny that it had been a marriage of convenience to allay doubts about Jackson and deflect publicity from the negative to the positive. "We will be expecting children but I won't be saying when. It's in the hands of the gods," Lisa Marie said. Her two children, Danielle and Benjamin, six and two respectively when the couple married, did not take to Jackson, reports alleged, even though he rarely disciplined them according to his wife.

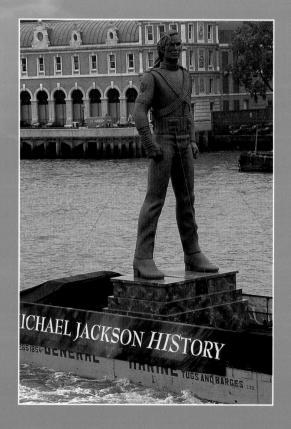

Nothing daunted by the accusations, Michael pushed out the boat to publicise *HIStory* when it was launched in June, 1995. Or rather, he had a huge statue of himself – much like those despotic heads of state have built to glorify their own achievements – tugged up the

River Thames in London on a barge, a piece of promotion repeated in other friendly capitals of the world. Perhaps not surprisingly in view of what had happened in the years preceding and during the recording of *HIStory*, the songs on it are often very angry. While it's true to say that the style – indignant lyrics and singing that calls for the words to be virtually spat out – had been developing since "Billie Jean" on *Thriller*, in the case of the lyrics, and *Bad* in the case of the vocal style, the overall feeling of many of the new tracks is of frustration stretched to bursting point.

HIStory came with a 52-page booklet stuffed with glowing words of support from Elizabeth Taylor, Steve Spielberg and the late Jackie Onassis, photographs snapped with four Presidents of the United States of America and Nelson Mandela, and a list of Awards he'd won that stretched over four pages. After all that had happened, he did not lack for influential friends. Although not as massive a seller as

"Thriller", "HIStory" none the less racked up several Number 1 hits amid the controversies. Protests about the lyrics of one song, "They Don't Care About Us", revolved around his use of the phrases "Jew me" and "Kike me". "I have come to understand over the past days that these words are considered anti-Semitic," he said, acknowledging that he had "seriously offended some people, which was never my intention, and for that I am deeply sorry." Later pressings of the record replaced the phrases with "Do me" and "Strike me".

And where did this leave his brothers and sisters, the kids he'd started out with back in Gary, Indiana? Only Jermaine had ever built up a genuine fanbase but as the years wore on, the treadmill of media interviews to promote each new album would find him being asked about Michael, not his own work. This grated. It did on all the Jacksons. "I do find it distressing that everybody wants to focus on Michael," Jermaine

once said. "Even though Michael is very talented, a lot of his success has been due to timing – and a little luck. It could just as easily have been me." Oh, really?

When Jermaine quit Motown to move to Arista in 1983, he had an immediate hit album, *Dynamite*, which had duets with Michael, Janet Jackson and Whitney Houston. The latter's duet also appeared on her first solo album which sold 15 million. Arista had hoped to release "Tell Me I'm Not Dreamin'", the duet with Michael, as a single but Epic refused clearance on their Jackson's vocal for fear of harming the sales of *Thriller* and its singles. "This would probably be my only Number One ever but I can't put it out," a miffed Jermaine said. By the release of his next album, *Precious Moments* (1986), Jermaine was confident enough to embark on his first solo tour since quitting the Jacksons 10 years earlier. "Don't Take It Personal" (1989), was followed by the LA/Babyface-produced "You Said" (1991).

But one of the biggest Jackson family successes beside Michael has been Tito Jackson's project, 3T: Tariano Adaryll, Taryll Arden and Tito Joe Jackson, his three sons who were first heard on the Free Willy soundtrack singing "Didn't Mean To Hurt You". Signed to Michael's MJJ label, and co-managed by Tito and Frank Dileo, the trio sang "What Will It Take" for Free Willy 2 and released a debut album, *Brotherhood* (1995) and started touring. They will not want for advisers.

But at present only Janet, the youngest child of Joe and Katherine Jackson who was born on August 16, 1966 and christened Janet Damita Jo, has come close to rivalling Michael's track record. She is not an outstanding live singer but a series of well-crafted records full of songs with catchy hooks and comparatively sparky lyric ideas caught a mood of self-confidence in life and love in the mid-eighties. She backed these up with well-staged dance routines on her tours, and she had already shown some promise as an actress by graduating from parts in long-running American soaps such as Good Times, Diff'rent Strokes and Fame to the lead role in the John Singleton film Poetic Justice.

Janet's first major appearance was in the family's cabaret show at the Las Vegas MGM Grand in 1974. She was eight. She later appeared in the 1976 CBS TV series, the Jacksons. In the early eighties, she signed to A&M records and released *Janet Jackson* (February, 1983). The album credits acknowledge no help at all from any of her brothers. but Marlon produced and co-wrote two of the nine tracks on 1984's *Dream Street*. The album also included an unlikely duet with Cliff Richard. Her next move was more inspired. Encouraged by John McClain, A&M's vice-president of A&R, she went to Minneapolis to work with producers Jimmy Jam and Terry Lewis, an increasingly hot team with hits by the SOS Band, Cherrelle and Alexander O'Neal, among others. *Control* (1986) was as much an agenda as an album. She had seen enough of control at close hand – Joe Jackson controlling his sons, Motown controlling the Jackson 5, and so on – to know what it meant and this was her bid to win control of her own life and career, and a call to everyone in a position to do the same for themselves to go for it. It was girl power some years before the Spice Girls were invented. Moreover, pairing Janet with the Jam-Lewis sound – crisp, jaunty, lite-funk Minneapolis rhythms to go with the crisp, catchy melodies – was a masterstroke creating the first Jackson solo recordings which seemed to owe nothing to the sound of Michael Jackson. *Control* sold 10 million as it reeled off six Top 50 hits before breaking out in a remix rash.

Three years on, after a follow-up, *Scandal*, was started and scrapped, she released *Janet Jackson's Rhythm Nation 1814* (1989), an anti-racist one-world sociopolitical manifesto (for the first three tracks at least; the rest is a good dance record), better focused than Michael's ideas on similar problems, but like him offering no solutions beyond let's all love one another. Perhaps there are no solutions other than that. With no less than seven hit singles, the album sold eight million as she set off on a world tour to rival her brother's *Bad*.

She rivalled Michael's recording contract, too, signing with Virgin for $32m in 1991. Her 1993 album, *janet.*, more consistent than *Rhythm Nation* but not as good as *Control*, was again produced by Jam-Lewis but had a glut of guests from rapper Chuck D to opera diva Kathleen Battle. There were seven singles and enough remixes to keep a small studio employed for a year culminating in the "janet. Remixed" album. Later came "Design Of A Decade 1986/1996", a 15-track "Best Of" collection plus two new songs.

All of this left her two sisters, LaToya Jackson (born LaToya Yvonne, May 29, 1956) and the Jacksons' first-born, Rebbie (that's Ree-bee) born Maureen Reilette on May 29, 1950), as stranded as a Marlon, Jackie or Tito. If Michael's scandals and Janet's breakout gave the press cause for, respectively, outrage and celebration, the hapless La Toya seemed destined for a mixture of pity and scorn. She scandalised her own family by posing nude for Playboy magazine and on September 5, 1989 married Jack

Gordon, a man between 18 and 22 years her elder depending on which partner's being honest about their birthdate. LaToya was not shy of the press and cracked the veneer of the Jacksons' as a happy, loving and well-adjusted family and, more damagingly, cast doubt on Michael's assertion that he was innocent of the charges of child-molestation. Her mother said La Toya would do anything for money and publicity.

Her albums suggest that without the family name she would never have been given a recording contract because her voice is expressionless, has very little range and no strength. Like Janet, she'd first performed with the brothers' act at the MGM Grand Hotel in Las Vegas in 1972. Her first album, *LaToya Jackson* (Polydor, 1981), featured a disco track, "Night Time Lover" (produced by and co-written with Michael). A second Polydor album, *My Special Love* (1982), had a dancefloor hit, "Shake Your Rump To the Funk". Moving to Private I, the *Heart Don't Lie* (1984) album got a lot of publicity off the back of Michael's success at the time with *Thriller*. Everyone wanted to know about her brother. Two years later came *Imagination*, then *You Blew It* (1988), a unhappily prophetic title. LaToya fled back to the family home in 1993 after allegations that husband Gordon beat her. Janet, too, had an unhappy first marriage to James DeBarge (that's right, of the DeBarges family whose band, Switch, Jermaine had got signed to Motown), a union which was annulled after just 14 months, James's drug problems proving too much for the young bride and marriage.

Rebbie, who had married at the age of 18 and set up home well away from the family, was persuaded into a recording studio on her own account by CBS, oddly enough when *Thriller* was selling by the container load. The title and best track of *Centipede* (1984) was written, produced and arranged by Michael. Her next album, *Reaction* (1986), was less lively and she was last heard in 1995 singing Bob Dylan's "Forever Young" on the soundtrack album of the Free Willy 2 movie.

Back on Planet Michael, the marriage between Neverland and Graceland, between Michael Jackson and Lisa Marie Presley ended as many had predicted. Scarcely had the nuptial spreads in the pages of *Hello!* magazine been pasted into the scrapbooks than Lisa Marie pronounced "irreconcilable differences" in the marriage. There seemed to be few moments of wedded bliss. The couple was soon spending Christmas and summer holidays apart – Lisa Marie went to Hawaii with her former husband and their two children – and arrived at and left shows like the MTV Video Awards separately. The divorce papers, which showed that the unhappy couple had separated on December 10, four days after Jackson had collapsed on stage during rehearsals for a TV show, were filed in January 1996. The marriage had lasted 18 months.

For the rest of the nineties so far, times have continued to be eventful for Michael Jackson. He unsuccessfully tried to buy The Royal Yacht Britannia for £25m, and has buddied up with Al-Waleed Bin Talal Bin Abdulaziz Al-Saud, a Saudi Arabian prince, to forge a partnership in the shape of Kingdom Entertainment, a company devoted "to defend family values and cultural diversity" and deplore "decadence and immorality" but also keen on building theme parks and hotels, making films and doing business in character licensing. He was a central guest at Elizabeth Taylor's 65th birthday party in Hollywood, a £1m bash held shortly before the actress underwent an operation on a brain tumour, where he sang "Elizabeth, I Love You", a specially-composed ballad with high sugar content.

Controversy was never far behind his actions, however. To film the video for his track "They Don't Care About Us" he and director Spike Lee went to the Santa Marta slum of Rio de Janeiro in Brazil. Local residents were pleased because his filming brought attention to the area's gross poverty. Local politicians, however, felt that it would be bad for the city's image. Dona Marta, a local drug baron, claimed that he received a pay-off from Jackson to film in the slum, which did not go down well with the local police, who said they had not been consulted about security for the visit. He came, he filmed, he left. The poor of Rio are still poor, its rich are still rich. Santa Marta remains, in the words of an inhabitant, "an island of misery surrounded by wealth".

In February, 1996, Jackson appeared at the Brit Awards in Earls Court, London, performing "Earth Song", another song off *HIStory* which kept The Beatles' "Free As A Bird" off the Number 1 spot over Christmas. The manner of his performance, using a stageful of small children to represent war victims and the poor, glorifying the Christ-like Jackson as a new messiah, did not go down too well, least of all with Jarvis Cocker, the lead singer of Pulp. Cocker, acting out "frustration and boredom'," he said, invaded the stage with a friend, cavorted, causing confusion among the children, gave the V-sign to the audience and cameras, and mooned before being hustled off stage. "It's farcical and ridiculous that Michael Jackson thinks people touching him will be instantly healed. He's totally out of touch with what is happening and he's got this image that he is the saviour of the world."

Epic, Jackson's record label, said their artist felt "sickened, saddened, shocked, upset, cheated, and angry, but is immensely proud that... the show went on despite the disgusting and cowardly behaviour of the two characters that tried to disrupt it." "The music industry allows him to indulge his fantasies... I just couldn't go along with it anymore," rejoined Cocker. "I didn't make physical contact with anyone as far as I can recall... All I was trying to do was to make a point and do something a lot of other people in the audience would have loved to have done if only they had dared." Charges against Cocker of assault on three children were dropped two weeks later and when he walked out of the West London police station, Jackson's fans threw eggs and flour at him. "You could have made a good Yorkshire pudding out of all that," Sheffield's star quipped.

Other music industry personalities at the Awards were equally affronted by Jackson's act. Former Roxy Music star turned producer and ambient music wizard Brian Eno took out an advertisement in Music Week, the UK music business's trade magazine, to give his opinion on Jackson's performance. "One of the most self-aggrandising and unpleasant things I have ever seen on a stage. It was as though a great balloon of pomp, hype, bad taste and flatulence had descended... Michael Jackson is a great musician and a great dancer. Unfortunately he is also turning into a great prat."

A few weeks later, Jackson appeared at the World Music Awards in Monaco, reprising the London spectacle and emerging from a silver globe to perform "Earth Song" in the company of some 35 children. There was no Jarvis Cocker on hand to temper the proceedings as children in the audience chanted, "Angel Michael".

And he got married, again, and became a dad. This time there was no doubt that the relationship amounted to an arranged marriage. Michael had met Debbie Rowe, a 37-year-old Australian nurse, some 15 years previously when he was attending the Hollywood skin clinic at which she worked.

The couple were married at a midnight ceremony in Sydney, Australia – Michael was touring there at the time, it's always nice to be able to mix business and pleasure – in November, 1996, less than a year after his divorce from Mrs Michael Jackson Mk I and with Mrs Michael Jackson Mk II already six months pregnant. Cue another picture spread in *Hello!* magazine. The pregnancy was widely-rumoured to be a financial deal with Rowe paid £300,000, although this was denied, as were suggestions that conception had been achieved by artificial insemination. It was further reported that DNA tests were carried out to ensure that Michael was the father.

Debbie duly gave birth to a boy, Michael Jackson Jnr, (7lb 10oz) on who was whisked away from his mother to live at the Neverland ranch while Mrs Jackson

recovered in hospital. Mrs Jackson Mk II was said to have signed away custody rights to her child for £1m. "Words can't describe how I feel. I have been blessed beyond comprehension and I will work tirelessly at being the best father that I can possibly be." He hoped people would respect the family's need for privacy. And then bidding for the first photo session of the infant with his dad started at a reported £350,000.

Jackson was said to be considering applying for British citizenship – one rumour had his manager Sandy Gallin contacting the British ambassador in Washington with a view to getting Jackson a knighthood or some similar type of gong, and while he was on the line was there any chance of Princess Diana appearing in the lavish HIStory booklet? – and was looking for a home in Scotland, perhaps a castle. One European home he did splash out on in the spring of 1996 was a huge 15th-century chateau in central France – 82 rooms, eight towers, moat, drawbridge, asking price £3.25m.

Energised by the birth of his son – and possibly very wary of all those school and college tuition fees looming on the horizon – Jackson got down to remixing the *HIStory* album prior to setting off on another world tour, the aptly-named *Burnin' Up The Dancefloor*. While his off-stage behaviour continued to generate all of the wrong sort of headlines – second wife Debbie Rowe complaining that he had whisked away their child before she had even the slightest glimpse of him after delivery – he was back on stage in the one area of life where he felt wholly in control. "I was raised on stage and I am more comfortable out there… When it comes time to get off, I don't want to. I feel like there are angels protecting me. I could sleep on stage. Once the music plays, it creates me."